A JOURNEY NOT EASILY FORGOTTEN

VICTORIA SELMAN

KP PUBLISHING COMPANY

ISBN: 978-1-960001-73-3 (Paperback)
ISBN: 978-1-960001-74-0 (Ebook)

Library of Congress Control Number:

Editor: KP Publishing Editing Services
Cover Design: Juan Roberts, Creative Lunacy
Literary Director: Sandra Slayton James

Published by:

KP Publishing Company
Publisher of Fiction, Nonfiction & Children's Books
Las Vegas, NV 89117
www.kp-pub.com

Printed in the United States of America

DEDICATION

This book is dedicated to my four wonderful sons, Josh, Joe, Jon and Joel. You have been my inspiration in writing this book. If it weren't for God allowing me to give birth to each of you, I would not have known the awesome power, protection, peace and provision of my sweet Heavenly Father. It is through the God-given responsibility of raising you that drove me to be the best mom to you that you deserved, and that included relying on God's wisdom and direction. In no way has it been an easy journey, but it certainly has been a fulfilling one.

Please know that every testimony in this book is a reminder to you, sons, that God has always and will always love and care for you. I love you with every fiber of my being, and God loves you even more.

Love, Mom

FOREWORD

"Jesus did many other things as well. If every one of them were written down, I suppose that even the whole world would not have room for the books that would be written." John 21:25 (NIV)

Books, books, books!

Would it not have been wonderful if we had a record of Jesus Himself written about Him - an autobiography by Jesus of Nazareth detailing events that have not been written down or preserved? One life. 33 years. All of it written down by the man who lived it - from his perspective. What would you or I pay for such a book? What is one life worth? Does one life really affect this whole world?

Whether it is you, or me, or Jesus, or Victoria Lee Selman, the answers to those questions are the same - It's priceless, everything, and YES!

Everyone has a book in them. Every life is valuable. Every life changes the world for good, bad, or a combination thereof. Every life matters, and every life should be preserved in the pages of a book for future generations to read and absorb the lessons that a life can teach. In fact, the Bible informs us that the details of our individual lives are all recorded in a book. God gives us value and records our lives in a book.

This is a wonderful autobiography by Victoria Lee Selman giving glory to God for the life he has given her, and walked with her each step of the way. It is a quick read but the messages and values in the stories are of eternal value, and full of inspiration and encouragement for any reader. The ups and downs and ebbs and flows in the trials and tribulations of her life lead to and expose the obvious intimate relationship that she has developed with her God, her Lord and Savior, and the Holy Spirit. The scripture that says to "trust in the Lord with all your heart" is fully demonstrated in her life, written down and manifested in both the little things and the big things that she trusted God for. She has truly learned the principle of not focusing on how big her problem is but on how big her God is to solve the problem. The underlying theme of every word on every page is that "God is good all the time, and he is able to do more than I can ever ask." As you read her stories you will be drawn into the same kind of relationship with God that she has.

God bless you, Victoria, and may this book go around the world to inspire and change lives and draw people to our awesome God!

Gary Colombo
Actor, Producer, Writer

CONTENTS

Contents

Chapter 17
Trust the Process   57

Chapter 1

THE PURE HEART IN GOD'S HANDS

As a little girl, my Heavenly Father had His hand on my life. I lived with my grandparents, which turned out to be such a blessing in many ways. We lived in a red house behind Orange Grove Baptist Church, and Reverend Amy was the pastor. I will never forget him because he always reminded me of my grandfather. On many occasions, my grandmother would give me a quarter and send me off to Sunday school and church. At the tender age of nine, I found myself walking down the aisle when the invitation to join the church was made. Tears began to flow. I didn't know what was happening at the time. but later in life I found out it was God tugging at my soft little heart. He truly had His hand on me, but, because I did not have the right guidance, I went on with life as usual.

Maybe you were raised in an unusual situation. Your parents may not have been there, but God saw to it that you were protected by someone who cared and nourished you with the love that was needed to form and shape you into the person you are today. My grandmother was that stabilizer in my life. She did not have the education like many others, but she instilled in me very valuable lessons that would prove to become an integral part of my life until this day. I once heard a great preacher say that you are complaining about how you were raised and that you were raised by someone other than your mom and dad. Be thankful that God had His hand on your life and protected you to put you where He wanted you to be. He always knows what's best for us, and in the end, He gets all of the glory.

Perhaps you are having that feeling of not being brought up in a normal family situation. Look at Queen Esther in the Book Of Esther. She was an orphan who had to be raised by her cousin Mordecai, who adopted her as his daughter. Her parents were killed when she was just a child, but God had a plan and purpose for her life. In the end, she had the most important role in saving her people from total desolation. Who would have known that she would be chosen "for such a time as this? Esther 4:14 (NKJV)

Chapter 2

YOUNG AND WILD

By the time I was twelve years old, my grandparents had moved to the south side of town and into our new house, which was directly across the street from my uncle and his family. I will always thank God for my Aunt. She tagged me along with my cousins to church and treated me like one of her own. She even taught me how to drive her 4-speed Volkswagen Bug, which I crashed several times. I had the privilege of singing in the Young Adult Choir. Then I went to high school. That is where my life started transforming from this sweet little innocent girl to someone very different and dark. I remember my Aunt asking me about going out and having fun with the other teenagers. So, I started making friends and going to parties. It proved to be not so good of an idea. Those parties turned into events that involved heavy drinking, smoking, and promiscuity.

In the meantime, the pastor of our church passed away, and a young, charismatic, and on-fire-for-God preacher took over. He got wind of the full gospel and, every week, began to preach salvation and being filled with the Holy Spirit.

And every week, I heard the call for salvation and wanted to go to the altar. Fear of getting up and going down in front of everyone gripped me like a lion that grabbed its prey, never letting go. I was literally terrified. What a huge risk I was taking on my eternal life!

So life went on as usual. By the time I got to college, I was on a sure path of self-destruction. I remember my freshman orientation like yesterday. Well, let me say most of it. I got so drunk that I passed out for a few seconds. After my first year of college, my grandmother bought me a brand new Chevy Chevette Scooter because I had started working and needed transportation. There were nights that my friends and I would drive to Fort Bragg in Fayetteville, North Carolina, to the NCO club looking for a fun time, which usually involved looking for guys. We would literally stay up all night. Pretty soon, however, I began to come to the end of myself. Terrible things started happening to me. I got pregnant not once but twice and had not one but two abortions. The promiscuity became such a casual event. I began to hate myself. That was when God got my attention.

I joined the gospel choir on campus during my second year at college. I learned how to sing and met lots of wonderful people. The choir consisted of two groups of students: those who were truly saved and those who were in the choir because they liked to sing. Meanwhile, I was not going to church, but once I began to have the desire to know Jesus, that all changed. All of those seeds that were sown into me while at my home church began to spring up, and before long, my desire to receive Jesus into my heart was far greater than the fear that once gripped me. So, one day, in my dorm room, I asked Jesus to come into my heart and be my Lord and Savior. It was like a heavy weight was lifted off my shoulders!

The first thing I did was to visit one of the sisters from the choir. I spent many hours with her that day. I'll never forget that beautiful fall Saturday. The next day, I went to the United Student Fellowship on campus and made my commitment public. At this point in my life, I didn't care who saw me or what they thought. I just knew I needed Jesus like never before and would do what it took to get to Him.

So, on October 7, 1983, I officially became a born-again believer.

To further prove my convictions, I totally surrendered everything to Jesus.

The desire to party and drink totally went away. I remember one of my close friends came to my school to pick me up to take her and her friends to a party at another college in town. I was so convicted in my heart at this point that I could not go in. I stayed in her car while they went in. Soon they took me back to my room. I never went to another party or drank again.

There comes a time in our lives that we must make decisions that will affect our lives. I made the decision to receive Jesus at the young age of nineteen, but it did not come without lots of battles for my life. The enemy wanted me for his glory, but God wanted me also. And in the end, my Heavenly Father won.

Do you need to make a major decision in your life? Maybe it's to accept Jesus or maybe you've already become born-again, and you are seeking God for answers to questions that will have a lasting impact. Whatever the situation, know that our Father God has all the answers, and He is just waiting for you to ask. In James 1:5, the New King James version of the Bible says, "If any of you lacks wisdom, let him ask God who gives generously to all without reproach, and it will be given him."

And if you are not born-again, know that He is just a prayer away. It is very simple. Just ask Him to forgive you of all of your sins and allow your Lord and Savior to come into your heart. And He will. Never be ashamed of your past. We all have one. You don't have to get right to get saved. Just receive Jesus, and He will make you righteous.

Chapter 3

THE JOURNEY BEGINS

There was one phone call I needed to make to my mother. She had given her life to the Lord when I was about eleven years old. She joined the Church of God in Christ in Washington, DC. There were many legalistic habits she had taken on, such as not wearing jewelry, make-up and choosing dresses over pants. I vowed I would never get saved after what I experienced at her church. There were lots of rules and regulations, but, at the same time, I saw lots of not so Christian-like activities. As a new believer, it was hard for me to see and try to comprehend.

Now, as a seasoned believer, I have come to realize it happens in all churches. Deep down inside, I knew that most of these people really loved the Lord, especially my mother! So I made a phone call, and sure enough the first thing my mom told me was the scripture from Deuteronomy 22:5:

> *"A woman shall not wear a man's garment, nor shall a man put on a woman's cloak, for whoever does these things is an abomination to the Lord your God."* (AMP)

I actually witnessed a young lady at my Mom's church turn down a basketball scholarship because she had to wear shorts, and it was against the church's beliefs.

Right after that phone call, I went straight to my campus pastor and consulted him. We ended up having a two-hour bible study. Later I thought about something. Out of all the movies I watched from the Old Testament, I never once saw men in pants. No one wore pants! Very interesting to say the least!

That same week I was at the bus station and a lady, for no apparent reason, came up to me to proclaim the Jesus-only doctrine. Wow! This doctrine declares that true baptism can only be "in the name of Jesus." The enemy had pulled out all his weaponry to try to distract me from the true gospel of Jesus Christ. I thank God He had the right people in place to guide me. That was a very important time in my life, and I was not going to let anything deter me.

It may be that you are a new believer and you are searching for guidance.

You may even have lots of questions about life and this new walk of yours. Search out a church that teaches straight from the Bible. Ask God to guide you to the place He wants you to be. Your growth in God should be your first priority. Surround yourself with other believers.

> *"Being confident of this very thing, that He who has begun a good work in you will complete it until the day of Jesus Christ."* Philippians 1:6 (NKJV)

Becoming mature in God does not happen overnight. In fact, it takes years of learning the ways and acts of God. The only way to find out is to read His Word daily if possible. Every answer pertaining to our lives can be found in the Bible.

Developing a relationship with the Father is so very important. That relationship is nourished through prayer. Prayer is simply talking to God and letting Him talk to you. Your journey as a new believer will be one filled with excitement, trials, victories, and lots of learning. I can tell you from experience that I do not regret my decision for Jesus. It has been the best thing that has ever happened to me!

Chapter 4

CLASS ACTION

A year after really learning and growing in the Lord, I began having the desire to get married. Why? Simply because I did not want to have sex outside of marriage. Because of my exposure to sex as a teenager, I did not want to fall. That was the wrong reason to tie the knot.

Nevertheless, I found myself in a relationship for eight months and down the aisle to getting married. As I went down the aisle, I'll never forget how I saw myself turning back, but I didn't. And so off I went to Northern Virginia to live happily ever after.

Not so! For the next six years of my life, it was a living hell! Fortunately, out of that union, I had four beautiful children: Josh, Joe, Jon, and Joel. But the warfare with my husband was so intense that I almost had a nervous breakdown. To tell the truth, I think I actually had one. I was always crying for no reason. I was so depressed that I couldn't take it anymore.

Was this the life as a Christian that I had envisioned? Of course not! In the previous chapter, I stated that this journey would be full of trials and lots of learning. Being newly married and somewhat young in Christ, I had not acquired the ability to control my anger. The only way I knew how to handle this was by attacking my husband physically when we argued. I felt so bad afterward because I knew it was wrong, and I didn't want to be that kind of person. Finally, I asked my heavenly Father to help me not react that way but to respond in love. I can remember the test came when an argument was in the making. I was sitting on the couch upstairs in the living room, and as the children's father approached me, I was talking to God in my heart. I was literally saying, "Here goes, Lord." I never reacted as I had previously, and from that day to this, I have never had another raging fit against another adult. That was my first real experience of that sort with the Father. If we truly want to be delivered from something, we will.

The word of God tells us in Ephesians 4:26-27,

> "Be angry and do not sin: do not let the sun go down on your anger, and give no opportunity to the devil." (NKJV)

In other words, we are all going to get angry; no one is excluded, but it is what we do with the anger that makes it a sin. I surely did not know how to deal with mine, and the outcome was shameful and caused lots of grief. Thank God I was sensitive enough to the Holy Spirit to yield to His unction. That is where we gain victory.

In the face of the trial, will we allow God's power to override those sinful attributes that we need to get rid of, and take on His nature? Don't get me wrong. It is indeed a process, but with much prayer and determination to please God, we can overcome:

> *"Now thanks be unto God, which always leads us in triumph in Christ, and diffuses the fragrance of His knowledge in every place."* 2 Corinthians 2:14 (NKJV)

Remember, class begins when we become Believers and does not end until we go home to be with the Lord. For every lesson, we must be active in God's Word to be victorious in every area of our lives.

Chapter 5

MY REFUGE

Throughout the duration of my marriage, there were so many times I wanted to give up and call it quits. Life within my household took on a life of its own that brought many weary days. I was a stay-at-home mom, and my daily care for my children and the laughter and play that came with it kept me going. I had learned as a new believer to spend time with God daily. I made a habit of saying a daily confession, also. It was important that I kept a tight schedule so I could have some kind of downtime or, as it is called these days, "me time." As all homemakers know, spending your time with children all day can warrant a little time to talk to an adult. Looking at something other than a kiddie show brought such comfort.

Nevertheless, I enjoyed each phase of my children's lives. As little toddlers, they loved to hear their bedtime story every night. Our routine was to read and pray before bedtime. Of course, they had to pick out the books. And that was alright with me as long as they were happy when I put them down for bed.

Life was getting harder and harder as my husband and I grew farther and farther apart. It became so difficult that I began to have a nervous breakdown. More often than not, emotional and verbal abuse can be more damaging than physical abuse. I couldn't take it anymore, so I planned my way of escape. I had one dollar left when I finished packing and putting our things in storage. It got really bad to the point where I had to call my girlfriend to come and get us. Out of the graciousness of her heart, she drove us to North Carolina the next morning. So there I was doing the unthinkable—something I never wanted for my children. I dreamed of having a beautiful life and family, but that was far from the present situation. I found myself a part of the dreaded statistic of being a single mom.

Yes, you may be a statistic of being a single parent, and, yes, you may feel like a failure, and once again, yes, your children are without their father in the home. Let's face it. Statistics say you are far from being alone with the rate of single parenthood increasing rapidly. The comfort I got was found in Psalms 68:5:

"Father of the fatherless and protector of widows is God in his holy habitation."(NKJV)

Your children's father may be living, but at 3 a.m., when your child is running a fever of 103 and vomiting, that's when you feel all alone. Ask me how I know. I've endured a child threatening to run away. How about working so hard that I got sick with strep throat year after year? Or working three jobs to make sure my children's needs were met. Not to mention carrying around a nine-year-old with a cast on his leg up to his thigh. Those are just a few things that I endured as a single parent.

God will never leave you nor forsake you. He is right there to catch every tear. He's waiting to wrap you in His loving arms and give you the peace you need through every situation and circumstance. Don't feel like you are a failure. We don't have failures. We have times of learning. Each setback is only setting us up for our success. The rejection you have endured is only protecting and redirecting you.

Let's take a look at some of our brothers from the Bible who endured similar circumstances. Pharaoh rejected Moses before allowing the children of Israel to be set free. Jeremiah was rejected by his people for prophesying to them, and those prophecies did not come to pass for at least 22 years. In the New Testament, Saul transformed into Paul, and he was rejected from the very beginning of his conversion until his death. And, of course, Jesus is the ultimate example of rejection. You know the cliché: every setback is a setup. Your mess is a message, and your test is a testimony.

Chapter 6

ABUNDANT FAVOR

Returning to my home church, Mt. Zion, in Durham, was like a breath of fresh air. It felt as if I had never left, as though God had closed up the time from when I left to the time I returned. Yet, the reality was starkly different—I came back with four babies, literally, between the ages of 4 and 3 months old. Praise and worship were wonderful, reviving my spirit. The more I attended church, the stronger my desire grew to join the praise team. In Virginia, I discovered my anointing as a praise leader. Singing was such an outlet and joy for me.

One night, I dreamt of people lined up along the railroad track near my childhood home. We were all waiting for Jesus to return while I sang worship songs. This vision solidified my calling. Before moving back to North Carolina, God opened many doors that nurtured my gift as a worshipper. He truly made room for my gift, and I knew without a shadow of a doubt that I was called to lead the church into His presence.

One of my deepest desires was to send my children to a Christian school. My grandmother insisted we receive assistance from social services because her retirement income couldn't support us all while I got back on my feet. I secured every benefit possible for my children. It didn't matter about me; I just wanted to ensure they were taken care of. With part of my welfare check, I enrolled and paid for Josh, my oldest son, to attend our church academy. That's how convicted I was about giving my children a Christian education.

Living across the street from the church academy was a blessing, especially since I had no transportation and could conveniently walk. Sometimes, I took the other children with me just to get them out of the house. However, crossing the street was dangerous because the parking lot entrance was in a curve.

One morning, as we were crossing, one of the children fell in the middle of the street. It was a terrifying moment, but by the grace of God, he was unharmed. My long-time friend witnessed the incident and began praying for us to get transportation. When the children's father and I separated, all I brought with me were our bare essentials and no transportation. I longed for peace and stability for my children, but I was desperate for a vehicle.

One of the church elders, who also ran a car dealership, handled transportation needs. A couple of days before Thanksgiving, I visited him, hoping to rent a car temporarily. My only income, outside of welfare, came from helping another pastor with his cleaning business. The elder, always willing to help, saw my desperation and made a phone call. I went back home and waited anxiously. As promised, he called back with news beyond my wildest dreams. Ephesians 3:20 says, "Now to Him who is able to do far more abundantly than all that we ask or think, according to the power at work within us" (NKJV). One of the deacons had a vehicle that he said I could have. This wasn't a piece of junk but a beautiful smoky gray four-door Cutlass Supreme! I received my blessing on Thanksgiving eve.

This was truly a testimony of God's goodness. Everyone in my family knew it had to be God because they knew I didn't have a steady job. They even acknowledged that it was God who blessed us. Reflecting on all the wonderful things God did for us brings tears to my eyes. Everything needed for the car, including tags, was provided. Now I could safely take my son to school without risking any of my children's lives.

Never doubt the provision of the Lord. Our Father takes pleasure in doing the seemingly impossible for His children. I have found over and over that sometimes you don't need any money—just the favor of God. As a single mother, there were many times I didn't have the necessary finances to meet our needs, but God always came through EVERY TIME! Consider the children of Israel in the wilderness. Not once did they go without their needs being met. Remember Elijah, fed by ravens during the drought? Jesus fed at least five thousand people with two fish and five loaves of bread, with leftovers to spare. Oh, what an awesome God we serve!

Chapter 7

THE BOOK OF ACTS

As time went on, I was faithful in my attendance at Mt. Zion. The next year I was hired as an assistant teacher at the academy. That was a challenge in itself, but once again God provided.

I had always wanted to be with my children, so this job allowed me to not only be with them in the same building, but also avoid paying for their tuition. The only expense I had was for was their books. Everything was looking up for my children and me. Slowly but surely we were getting on our feet.

One of the sisters who worked in the academy desperately needed transportation. She was also a single mom. She stepped out by faith and went to the local Ford dealership. God blessed her to get a brand new Ford Escort. At the Wednesday night Bible study, she testified about how God favored her in getting her car. Suddenly, the same elder who helped me get my first car, stood up and offered to pay her first payment. What??? Then another person stood up, and still another until her car was totally paid off!

Not only that, the pastor made a request for anybody with a need to come down to the altar. I needed to pay for my second-oldest son's weekly preschool tuition. And God provided! One of the men in the church offered to pay my son's tuition each week. And that night, I went home with a bag full of cash. My grandmother could not understand why I gave "my money to that church," as she called it, but out of obedience to my heavenly Father, I always paid my tithes. When I poured all the money God had blessed me with on the kitchen table, my response was, "This is why I pay my tithes and offering."

Truly the Book of Acts was in operation that night. This was the raw modern day version being manifested right before our eyes. Acts 4:34-35 says, "There was not a needy person among them, for as many as were owners of lands or houses sold them and brought the proceeds of what was sold and laid it at the apostle's feet and it was distributed to each as any had need."(NKJV)

I dare to say that if every church had this system in place for legitimate needs in the body of Christ, the love of God would be manifested. This would be an expression of God's hand extended to those who, from time to time, feel hopeless and helpless. It is only through His love that this can be done. For the most part, I believe far less believers in the body of Christ would struggle to have their needs being met.

Chapter 8

REDEEMED AND RESTORED

As good of a blessing as the Cutlass Supreme was, it eventually died while I was going to an event one Sunday evening. I had to have transportation because of all the activities I was involved in. There was a couple I was really good friends with who always babysat my children while I went to rehearsals and singing engagements. They offered to accompany me to Fayetteville, North Carolina, to buy something economical to drive. I ended up purchasing a black Toyota Camry. Within 2 weeks, the transmission went out and the dealership would not help me purchase a new one. I had to shovel out nine-hundred dollars!

This sister was not a happy camper! The car gave me so much trouble that I decided to return it even though I owed seven hundred dollars. To make matters worse the dealer stated that there would be a judgment against me, and it would show up on my credit report. At this point, I didn't care. I just wanted to get rid of the lemon! My exact response to God was, "God, you know that's not even right!" Many of the sisters at church were getting brand new vehicles from the local Ford dealership. So I decided to step out by faith and take a visit.

While applying for the car, the sales manager said there was a $700 judgment on my credit, but it did not affect my credit enough for me not to qualify for the vehicle. God came through, and my family and I were once again blessed with decent transportation! This time it was a brand new Ford Escort! It felt so good to have something to transport my children in without being concerned that we were going to be stranded somewhere.

Later on in that year, I trusted in God to help me buy a house. There were many first time homebuyer programs to take advantage of, and that's what I did, but in the back of my mind, I knew that $700 judgment would appear. With much apprehension I got my credit report through one of the counselors, and surprisingly discovered that the judgment was gone. Not only was it gone, but I found out that the dealership who sold me the lemon was out of business. This was truly a miracle from God. He cleared my debt!

God cares so much for us that He will cover and protect us even when we make dumb mistakes. The Father not only wants to provide for His children, but as He says in Isaiah 45:2, "I will go before you and make the crooked places straight; I will break in pieces the gates of bronze and cut the bars of iron."(NKJV) Isaiah 41:10-11 in the Amplified says, "Do not fear (anything), For I am with you; Do not be afraid, for I am your God. I will strengthen you, be assured I will help you; I will certainly take hold of you with My righteous right hand."

So my sister and brother, trust God for your every provision. He is right there to meet every need even when we mess up. Be assured that what loss we experience, our sweet Heavenly Father is always ready to restore us and give us back better than what we originally lost.

Chapter 9

THE PROTECTOR

While working at the academy, we always had our summers off. So I decided to get a job selling alarm systems. My partner was a pregnant mom who was well over half way to her due date. One day it was very hot and humid, so I suggested she stay in the car while I knocked on doors in one of the neighborhoods.

It had just rained, so the atmosphere was really sticky. I had to walk down a long driveway to get to the door of the house I was approaching. Midway in the driveway, I suddenly heard a word ring loud in my spirit – SNAKE! So I started looking down as I was walking. I got up to the porch and rang the doorbell. As I looked down in the flower bed, there so peacefully and quietly camouflaged was a medium sized reptile beautifully set in an array of colorful foliage. I calmly did an about face and quickly walked back to my car!

I thank God for His divine protection. Not only did He protect me, but He warned me! Our Father loves us so much that He will warn us of danger. One example that comes to mind is how Joseph, Jesus' earthly father, was warned several times in dreams to protect the baby Jesus.

Chapter 10

MY SHELTER IN THE TIME OF NEED

In the meanwhile, my family needed a place of our own. It was becoming increasingly difficult to live with my grandmother. She was doing the best she could to help me with the children, but I knew it was hard on her. So I began to pray for a place of our own.

My great aunt resided in a 2 bedroom apartment near the local university. A year or so after I moved to North Carolina, she had a stroke and was unable to take care of herself. There was paralysis on the left side of her body. As a result, she moved to a special care facility. The apartment was just sitting there with all the utilities on. Nothing had been moved or changed since she left. The family knew they had to do something with the apartment.

Behold a miracle was manifested! My grandmother asked me if I could handle paying for the apartment. Of course I said yes! I was going to do whatever I had to do to make it happen. Not many days hence, we were moving into the apartment. How good was God? We didn't have to turn on any utilities. We didn't have to buy any food. We even had toothpaste and other needed toiletries. All we had to do was move in.

With God, "nothing shall be impossible." (NKJV, Luke 1:37) "And my God will supply every need of yours according to his riches in glory in Christ Jesus." (NKJV, Philippians 4:19). Before long we were all moved into our own 3-bedroom apartment. God was really showing himself mightily for my family!

To further provide for my family, I helped run an afterschool program in addition to working at the academy. I became really good friends with one of the parents who had a little girl the same age as my second oldest son. We were pretty close by the end of the school year. She was a single mom in the military and was about to do a tour in Japan. However, she had to go to a five month class in Georgia. At this point, I had decided to homeschool the boys. She did not want to take her daughter with her for five months, enroll her in school, and then have to pull her out. So she asked if I would keep her and homeschool her along with my children. Without any hesitation I agreed.

Two positive situations came out of this arrangement. First, to my surprise, it was not so nice for my oldest son. He did not like the transition of having another child whom his mother had to cater to just a little more than she catered to him. It was really cute to see how he strived to keep my attention. If I held my girlfriend's daughter's hand, he had to hold my hand as well. Little notes were written to Mommy about his time being taken. He showed me that he needed me just as much.

Second, as it turned out, this little girl had a godfather who was also in the military and would come to check on her on occasion. This guy was as big as Dwayne Johnson, the Rock! There was not one ounce of fat on his body, but he was as gentle as a lamb. I guess you would say he was a gentle giant. He turned out to be a savior, as I'll explain later.

It was a nice change of pace to have a little girl in the house. God had blessed me with my own place in order to be a blessing to another single mom. If I continued to live with my grandmother, I would not have been able to be a blessing to my girlfriend.

Chapter 11

ROOM FOR
THE GIFT

As time progressed, a new minister of music was hired and changes were being made in the music department at church. One day while I was on my lunch break, I stepped in the sanctuary and took a seat while the new team was rehearsing. I told God in my heart that I sure wish I could sing with them. Not more than 48 hours later, the minister of music called me into his office. He proceeded to tell me that he had a dream that he asked me to be on the praise team. Oh my goodness! That was a dream come true. God answered the prayers of my heart. What was so awesome was that I never spoke a word to anyone or said anything out loud. That desire was burning deep within me, and God honored it.

That began a series of opportunities to do weddings and special programs as well as the normal services during the week. We even did a live recording!

No matter where you are, God will see to it that your gift is made known. When we have our hearts in the right place with the Lord, and we are faithful to Him, He will use us. The gift that He has placed in us from the foundation of the world never leaves. When we choose to allow that gift to lie dormant, we grieve the Father's heart. Not only does it sadden Him, but we rob many of receiving a blessing from God through us. God told Jeremiah that before He formed him in his mother's womb, He knew him and ordained him a prophet to the nations (NKJV, Jeremiah 1:5). As Jeremiah received his gift, so I received mine!

Chapter 12

CONTINUED FAITHFULNESS

My boys were growing and playing year round sports which included Pop Warner football, recreational basketball, and track. Boy, were we a busy family!

A car wasn't sufficient for what we needed as a family anymore. So, just as we looked to God for our home, we began to pray for a larger vehicle. The Holy Spirit told me to instruct the children to fast, pray and sow a seed. So we poured all of our money that we had saved in the middle of the floor to take to church and offer it to God for our van. When I took the money to the office and told the clerk I wanted to sow a seed, she asked where I wanted to sow it. I responded that it didn't matter. I just wanted to sow the seed. My heart's desire for my children was to make God practical to them, not just be someone who we hear about in church, but to actually experience his presence, goodness and love for us as a family. Allowing them to sow a seed, to fast and to pray showed them that God honored their prayers as children just like He did for everyone else.

Once again God used the same elder that blessed us with our first car to be a blessing to us. I was able to buy a brand new van from him, but there was one catch. I had to get to Fort Wayne, Indiana to get it from the Ford dealership there. Oh Boy! How was that going to happen? To make a long story short, my girlfriend's daughter's godfather (the Rock) was going to Illinois and Indiana was not far from where he had to go. So out of the goodness of his heart, he agreed to bring our van back.

Hallelujah! God did it! I did not have to spend one dime on shipping or buying an airline ticket to go get the vehicle and drive it back. My sweet heavenly Father just dropped the favor right in my lap. When the Rock got there, he caught the flu and had to stay for about a week longer than he wanted to. That was the longest week I had experienced in a long time. The following Saturday that he was due to come back, we kept going back to our apartment between the boys' basketball games to see if he had arrived. Finally, the last time we came home, the van was backed in the parking space in our complex. We were so happy! It was truly a dream come true for us.

Is there something you need from God? I suggest finding scriptures that support your belief in God and what you need from Him. In addition, begin sowing seeds toward that. That is, give offerings for what you are asking. Whenever I give an offering, I never give without purpose. In other words, each time, I name my seed. I attach my seed to what I am trusting God for. Countless times I have seen our Father honor my seed sown. I never spoke against what I wanted from God.

For instance, if you are renting a room in a house and you are believing in God for your own house, always thank God for your house, especially when things are not going your way. Never complain about your situation, but always give thanks. You must choose to trust God and do good. (NKJV, Psalms 37:3)

Chapter 13

THE FAITH RESTS

After teaching in the Academy for several years, I decided to home school my children. It proved to be challenging as well as rewarding. I remember so clearly standing on Scripture: "For in it the righteousness of God is revealed from faith for faith." (NKJV, Romans 1:17) That is, the just shall live by faith.

One of my friends asked me how I was providing for my family. I boldly proclaimed that scripture. Other parents in our homeschool group couldn't figure out how I was able to homeschool my children and survive. When I would take my children to enrichment once a month, people would always refer to my husband. I would then have to tell them that I was not married. You see, I drove a brand new van and didn't work. It was only God who made a way and got the glory. By God's grace, not one time did we go without food. All of our bills were always paid.

Pretty soon I began a couple of businesses that would begin to take up my time. I cleaned houses and did custom sewing as a way to make extra money. It was getting increasingly difficult to properly educate my children. At that time, the North Carolina legislature passed a bill to allow parents to receive vouchers to put children in the private school of their choice as opposed to going to public school. Our church just so happened to be one of the locations to perform the lottery. I knew I wanted my children in a Christian homeschool academy around the corner from our complex that was very reputable. I also knew I didn't have the financial means to pay for 4 children, but I did have God!! So with faith, I put my name in the lottery. I really didn't think I would get chosen.

I was so exhausted the night of the drawing that I didn't have the energy to go to the lottery drawing. I literally fell asleep. That night I received a phone call that my name had been drawn. Glory to God!! He is so faithful! Once again my Father provided for us. Now I was able to put my children in the home school academy for free! When we delight ourselves in the Lord and put Him first in our lives, "He will give us the desire of our hearts."(NKJV, Psalm 37:4a)

I truly believe that it was no coincidence that I was asleep during the lottery drawing. It was like a prophetic act of my trust in God. He wants us to rest in knowing that He is behind the scenes working. "Let us therefore strive to enter that rest, so that no one may fall by the same sort of disobedience."(NKJV, Hebrews 4:11). I had to come to this place of rest and peace to see the hand of God move on my behalf. Rest is so important physically and spiritually. To reiterate Hebrews 4:11, The Passion Translation says, "So then we must give our all and be eager to experience this faith-rest life, so that no one falls short by following the same pattern of doubt and unbelief."

I encourage you to read the entire chapter of Hebrews 4. It gives us an example of how the children of Israel doubted God and walked in unbelief. Let's heed the Word of the Lord through His Word. Trust God and rest in Him, my friend. He has you covered!

Chapter 14

PEACE RULES

During this time, I had entered into a relationship with a gentleman that I believed would become my husband. Without going into detail, it was a very tumultuous road. Nonetheless, I truly believed this was the "one." I have learned through my experiences that if everything is not lining up with the word of God, it is not God's will.

There were many issues where I compromised my faith at the expense of my family's peace and well-being. If it takes you away from God in any way, form, or fashion, it is not from God. At any rate, I continued the relationship. We were planning to get married. He was divorcing his wife because she had left him. We found a house in another city and the children and I moved in while he was finishing up the business with the sale of his house. His house sold before we had a chance to get married, which meant he had to move into the house that the boys and I were already living in.

Well, that wasn't going to work for me because I was not going to live in the same house with a man in front of my children and not be married! He had no choice but to move in, and everything changed. I chose to sleep in my van! No fun! I had absolutely no peace at this point. I didn't know what to do. It was a very awkward time for me. I knew I was out of the will of God

At the time, I was making a decent income with my cleaning and sewing businesses. I began to look in the newspaper for places to live. My plan was to rent a used double-wide mobile home. Those were pretty reasonably priced. I saw an ad that I responded to and made plans to check it out. At the time, the boys were in summer youth camp for a few days at church. I remember telling the boys, when I dropped them off, to pray for me since the youth were fasting and praying.

I met with a salesman and was asked to come back on Monday with a $500 check. So that Monday I picked the boys up from their camp and arrived at the scheduled time. The salesman took us to a room with a large conference table. As I looked around while waiting, I began to sense something unusual was about to happen. I let the boys know what I was feeling. By this time the salesman came in with a packet of papers and proceeded to tell me that I qualified for a brand new house. Just to interject, I didn't have a regular full-time job. I was only making money from my businesses which was not steady income, but at that point, I was bringing in a decent amount. The salesman let us pick out the one we wanted.

There was an island in the kitchen of the house we chose. I was overwhelmed with what God had done for us! Immediately, I told the boys to grab hands and we prayed and thanked God for our blessing in front of the salesman. Once again, God took care of us and got the glory!

I found when there is no peace in your heart about a situation, that is not the time to move forward; it is the time to seek the face of God for direction. Colossian 3:15 has become one of the scriptures that I have really learned to stand on. In the Amplified, it says, "Let the peace of God (the inner calm of one who walks daily with Him) be the controlling factor in your hearts (deciding and settling questions that arise)." Possibly, you're in a situation where you have no peace. Perhaps it is God tugging at your heart to make the necessary changes that need to be made to bring you into a place of walking in his perfect will. God gives us a free will, but, as a believer, we learn that His perfect will always overrides His permissive will.

We cannot receive the full manifestation of the Lord's blessings in our lives when we do life our way. He wants and knows what's best for us. So why not trust Him today?

Chapter 15

RELIEF IS ON THE WAY

We finally moved into our new house. Oh, what a feeling of relief and peace! God somehow always provides. I had to put my children in public school. This was not my desire, but at this point, I had no choice. Boy, were they happy. No more uniforms!

At the same time, I needed a good job to take care of my family and me. It was really rough trying to manage a new house. Because I was living so far away from where my cleaning job was, I decided to get a local job. I was hired through Manpower at a local warehouse and really made some good friends, but it was still a little rough financially. So I decided to apply to the post office. I took the test and passed. Soon I was offered a position. What a relief!

My first day on the job I was assigned to Route 13. I was trained for the first week and released to do the route by myself the next week. To say the least, my first day was quite interesting. While navigating through my route, I came to a cul-de-sac and realized I delivered the wrong mail to 3 of the boxes. The houses in the middle of the cul-de-sac had long steep driveways. As I was correcting my mistake on foot, out came a huge black dog, maybe a Labrador retriever. Needless to say, I was terrified but did not panic. Initially, he was at the end of the driveway, but as I kept moving, he galloped toward the middle of the cul-de-sac. I had two choices. I could run for my life, or use what I knew and that was to command him to stop in the name of Jesus! I chose the latter. And glory to God it worked! It was as if God put super glue on the dog's paws as the dog was stuck in that position.

His head moved but his body was immobile. I imagined the dog was wondering what happened as he looked around in such deep curiosity!

I drove off praising God for protecting me once again! No matter what I went through on my new job, it was a welcome relief for us money-wise. Finally, I could exhale and begin to move toward the life God had for my family. I was overwhelmed with what God did for us!

Chapter 16

THE ENCOURAGEMENT

There are many more stories that I have, but these stories are just a snippet of the faithfulness of God to my family. I pray that, as you read through each chapter, you were encouraged in some way. It is a lifelong goal of mine to pour God's love into the younger single mothers and fathers of our society. Make no mistake about it; God allows us to go through tests and trials to grow us, make us, mold us, and shape us. Just know that God wants to use what you go through to help someone else.

When I see younger parents these days and some of their situations, it makes me so happy when I can give advice and counsel out of my own experiences. We go through nothing in vain. James 1:2-4 in the Passion Translation says, "My believers, when it seems as though you are facing nothing but difficulties, see it as an invaluable opportunity to experience the greatest joy that you can! For you know that when your faith is tested, it stirs up power within you to endure all things. And then as your endurance grows even stronger, it will release perfection into every part of your being until there is nothing missing and nothing lacking."

Chapter 17

TRUST THE PROCESS

Today I am happily married to the man of my dreams. However, my sweet Heavenly Father had to teach me that He is a jealous God, and He is to be first in every area of my life. Before meeting my husband, God told me that in order for me to have the man of my dreams make me the happiest woman in the world, He had to first make me the happiest woman in the world. So, what did I do? I became very intimate with God. It was so sweet that I began to refer to Him as my "sweet Heavenly Father." Soon after, I met my husband.

Always trust the process of what God is doing in your life. Then learn to treasure your journey that will not be easily forgotten.

INVITATION TO SALVATION

Have you asked God to come into your heart to be your Lord and Savior? It is a very simple process. The Father loves you so much that He sent His son Jesus to die on the cross for your sins. It doesn't matter what you have done in the past. Jesus' sacrifice on the cross is enough to cover everything that you have ever done to offend our God. He's just waiting for us to receive the precious gift of salvation and an eternal life with Him. "For God so loved the world that He gave His only begotten Son, that whosoever believes in Him should not perish but have everlasting life. For God did not send His Son into the world to condemn the world, but that the world through Him might be saved." (NKJV, John 3:16-17). To be saved you must believe in your heart that God raised Jesus from the dead and confess with your mouth the Lord Jesus." (NKJV, Romans 10:9). It's that simple. If you are ready to be born again just pray the prayer below:

Lord Jesus, I have sinned against you. I am tired of this life and want a new life with you. I believe that God raised you from the dead and I confess with my mouth that you are Lord. I ask you to come into my heart and save me from my sins. Thank you for saving me!

Welcome to the family of God!

ACKNOWLEDGMENTS

Thanks to my many friends and family that encouraged me and had such an influence in my life to write this book. There were so many people who saw the gift in me and believed in me. In particular, my godfather, Bishop Milton Herring, Dena Rentrope, Pastor Tim Roberson, Karen Adams, Carla Thompson, Gary Colombo, Bridgette Banks, members of Lifehouse Worship Center in Irvine, California and many others.

I could not have written this book without your prayers, prophetic words and edification. But there is one person who has recently come into my life that I must acknowledge and that is my wonderful husband, George Selman. He has always encouraged me and set himself in agreement with me in what I believe God has called me to do. From day one he has continuously supported me. And for that I am forever grateful. And to my mother, who is now gone on to be with the Lord, I will always cherish her encouragement, her faith and example of love.

ABOUT THE AUTHOR

Victoria Selman, born in Durham, North Carolina, was lovingly raised by her grandparents in a structured and nurturing environment. From an early age, Victoria was drawn to the Baptist church near her home, where she felt a profound spiritual calling at just nine years old. Despite the simplicity of her early life and the lack of spiritual guidance, her faith journey took a significant turn at nineteen following a series of traumatic events, leading her to commit her heart to Jesus fully.

Victoria's gift for singing, evident since she was five, blossomed into a lifelong ministry. After the birth of her first child, she embraced praise and worship, contributing to several recording projects, including two singles of her own. Her passion for music remains a cornerstone of her faith expression.

After marrying, Victoria pursued theological studies at a local Bible college, recognizing her calling to teach God's word. Now a dedicated chaplain, she leads Bible studies at Florence McClure Women's Prison and her local church, where she shares her deep love for writing through journaling, Bible studies, and devotionals.

In her spare time, Victoria enjoys crafting and runs her own business, Sew Sewful Designs, delighting in creating gifts for her grandchildren and friends. She is also an avid fitness enthusiast, engaging in activities like pickleball, badminton, ping-pong, racquetball, hiking, and enjoying nature walks.

After raising her four children as a single parent, Victoria returned to college, earning a Bachelor's degree in Business Administration with honors. She is now remarried to Pastor George Selman, and together they serve their community through Oil Fields Ministries. Victoria's dedication to community service is particularly focused on impacting the lives of young women, especially single mothers. Her commitment to serving others is driven by a deep conviction to fulfill God's will in her life.

www.ingramcontent.com/pod-product-compliance
Lightning Source LLC
Chambersburg PA
CBHW051009140626
46546CB00016B/1379